Daring Sea Captains

395

De magnitudine Noruagici Serpentis, & aliorum.

An Italian woodcut dated 1555. The Latin inscription reads: "Concerning the size of the Norwegian serpent, and others [of its kind]." For centuries, people had been convinced that sailors would be eaten by monsters like this.

A Pull Ahead Book

Daring Sea Captains

Marcia Scott

Lerner Publications Company • Minneapolis, Minnesota

ACKNOWLEDGMENTS: The illustrations are reproduced through the courtesy of: p. 2, Rare Book Division, New York Public Library, Astor, Lenox & Tilden Foundations; pp. 5, 9, 35, 40, The Library of Congress; pp. 6, 18, 20, 23 (top & bottom), 25, The National Maritime Museum; p. 7, Antikensammlungen, Munich; p. 8, J.C. Bosmel, courtesy of the Tahiti Tourist Board, Papeete; p. 11, Dixson Galleries, The Mitchell Library, New South Wales; p. 12, National Portrait Gallery; p. 14, The Parker Gallery, London; p. 15, The Field Museum of Natural History; p. 17, F. W. Beechey, *Narrative of a Voyage to the Pacific*, Thomas Davison, Whitefriars; pp. 26, 29, 31, *The Voyages of Joshua Slocum*, edited by Walter Teller, Rutgers University Press; pp. 32, 48, 51, Independent Picture Service; pp. 33, 38, Royal Geographic Society, London; pp. 41, 45 (top), John F. Kennedy Library; p. 42, National Archives; pp. 45 (bottom), 66, 67, United States Navy; pp. 47, 53, Rand McNally; pp. 54, 55, 70, 71, 78, United Press International; pp. 56, 58, 59, 61, Les Requins Associes, Groupe Cousteau; p. 63, National Geographic Society; p. 64, William R. Anderson; p. 73, Public Relations Office, Suva; p. 77, South American Travel News.

LIBRARY OF CONGRESS CATALOGING IN PUBLICATION DATA

Scott, Marcia.
Daring sea captains.

(A Pull Ahead Book)
SUMMARY: Biographical sketches of nine famous seamen: William Bligh, Horatio Nelson, Joshua Slocum, Ernest Shackleton, John F. Kennedy, Thor Heyerdahl, Jacques-Yves Cousteau, William R. Anderson, and Robin Lee Graham.

1. Shipmasters—Juvenile literature. 2. Seamen—Juvenile literature. [1. Seamen] I. Title.

G175.S38 910'.45'0922[B][920] 72-3592
ISBN 0-8225-0465-0

International Standard Book Number: 0-8225-0465-0
Library of Congress Catalog Card Number: 72-3592

contents

Sir Francis Drake

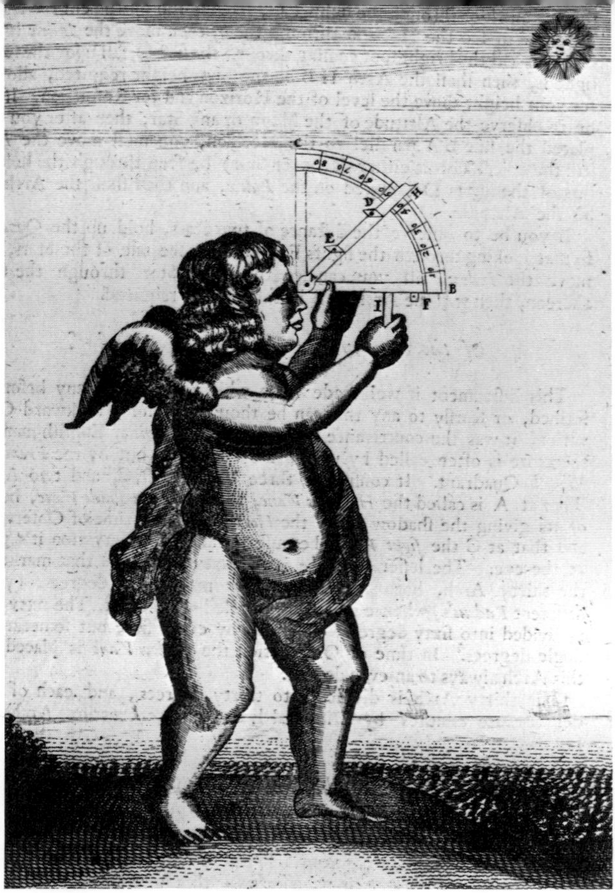

A celestial navigator uses the sun and a sextant to plot his course.

Early Seamen

There were daring sailors long before Columbus. It took boldness in the early days for man to venture beyond the sight of land. People believed that all sorts of terrors waited for the foolish ones who put out to sea. But some brave men dared to take the chance. For them, the sea was a challenge.

The origins of boat building and seafaring date back to 10,000 B.C. in Egypt. The Egyptians had trade routes on the Red Sea, the Indian Ocean, and the Mediterranean Sea.

The Phoenicians, neighbors of the Egyptians, were the most famous ancient seafarers. They lived on the eastern shore of the Mediterranean. These "gypsies of the sea" were the first mariners who dared to sail beyond the sight of land. They were also the first to use the North Star as a guide for sailing at night.

The Phoenicians traded and explored throughout the Mediterranean, bringing back precious stones. In 1100 B.C., they ventured through the Straits of Gibraltar into the uncharted Atlantic Ocean and around the coast of Africa. To discourage Greeks and other rival traders, the Phoenicians often invented stories about terrible sea monsters and dangerous rocks that they had seen in their travels.

An ancient Greek ship might have looked like this, but without the grapevines.

Pytheas (PITH-ee-us), a Greek astronomer and geographer, was the earliest of the great explorers. In 325 B.C., he set sail from the Greek colony of Massalia (now Marseille, France), with over 100 men. Pytheas and his men slipped past a Phoenician blockade at Gibraltar and entered the Atlantic, which no Greek had ever done before. Fascinated by the unknown, Pytheas sailed north of the British Isles into an area that the Greeks had always considered lifeless and frozen. There, he came upon a huge island where the midnight sun rested on the edge of the ocean, and where plant and animal life thrived. Pytheas called this land Thule, meaning "afar." (The location of Thule has never been verified.)

Other, more primitive societies were also lured by the sea. Ancient South Sea Islanders learned to build canoes and to navigate them by the sun and stars. They island-hopped to find food for their people. A Polynesian named Kupe, sailing from Otaheiti (Tahiti) in a dugout canoe, discovered New Zealand in 950 A.D. He had traveled 3,500 miles.

A Tahitian dugout canoe. For centuries, native sailors have skillfully navigated these frail-looking craft over vast stretches of ocean.

Another group of seamen were the Vikings, or Norsemen. These daring sea raiders sailed across the mysterious Atlantic in their swift high-prowed ships. They had no compass or chart. Eric the Red explored Greenland, giving it that name to attract settlers. His son, Leif Ericson, who was later known as Leif the Lucky, landed on the coast of North America in 1000 A.D. He called it Vinland, meaning "wineland."

Leif Erickson and his crew sight land.

Four centuries after the Vikings' voyages, European countries sought a sea route to India and the treasures of the Orient. The Age of Discovery had begun. Bartolomeu Dias rounded the southern tip of Africa, which was later named the Cape of Good Hope. Dias had to turn back because his sea-weary men refused to sail further on the stormy seas at the Cape. But his experience was valuable to another Portuguese mariner, Vasco de Gama, who was the first to reach India by sea.

The Spaniard Ferdinand Magellan sought to find a westward route to Asia. At the tip of South America he discovered a passage which is now called the Straits of Magellan. Then he traveled across the Pacific to the Philippines, where he was killed in a battle with the natives. Magellan's crew, however, completed the first voyage around the world, beating the rival Portuguese. Sir Francis Drake and many others followed in Magellan's wake.

Two centuries later, Captain James Cook of Great Britain charted the South Pacific. He made three long voyages there, starting in 1768. In 11 years Cook charted thousands of miles of land and ocean from the ice islands in the south to the Bering Straits in the Arctic. He proved that there was no southern continent which could support life, and that a sea passage over the top of the world was impossible. During Cook's third voyage, he stopped at the Sandwich (Hawaiian) Islands, which he had discovered earlier. There, he was killed by natives.

The death of Captain James Cook

At the close of the 18th century, explorers had charted most of the world's oceans. Men began to make use of the sea, and they ceased to fear it as they had in earlier days. Governments knew that great navies could protect them in times of war. Modern traders discovered that fortunes could be made with fleets of merchant ships. Ocean travel was still somewhat hazardous and uncomfortable, but it did become a more commonplace experience. The fearful legends of the past had been disproved or explained, and daring sea captains of the modern age sailed with new confidence. But the sea adventures of the modern age were no less thrilling than the adventures of the past.

Captain William Bligh
(1754-1817)

The career of Captain William Bligh has been a subject of debate for many years. Some historians have pictured Bligh as the cruel and ill-tempered captain of the *Bounty.* Others have made him a hero. The truth probably lies somewhere in between.

Bligh began his career as a seaman early in life. In 1776, when Bligh was 23 years old, he served as sailing master of the *Resolution.* Captain Cook commanded this ship on his final voyage to the Pacific. The expedition's main mission was to find a Northwest Passage in the Arctic. Ice forced Cook and his crew to turn back, but Bligh gained experience and proved his ability as a navigator and surveyor.

After the Cook expedition, Bligh was promoted to captain. In 1787, he set out from England on the *Bounty*, bound for the South Pacific. His task was to bring young breadfruit trees from Otaheiti (Tahiti) to the British colonies in the West Indies. There the breadfruit trees would be planted and their fruit used as cheap food for slaves.

Bligh had planned to reach the South Pacific by sailing around the continent of South America. But stormy weather off the tip of South America forced him to turn around and take a route past Africa instead. The voyage was a long one, and the crew grew restless aboard the small, uncomfortable ship. Finally, a year after leaving England, the *Bounty* reached Otaheiti. Unfortunately, Bligh and his men had arrived during the wrong season to dig up the breadfruit trees. They had to stay in Otaheiti for five months in order to complete their task.

The first day after leaving Otaheiti, the crew complained that their small supply of water was being wasted on the breadfruit trees. There was also a quarrel over coconuts. Bligh accused Fletcher Christian, the master's mate, of being a thief. That night, on April 28, 1789, Christian and three others seized and bound Bligh while he was sleeping in his cabin. Bligh pleaded with Christian to reconsider his terrible deed.

"'Tis too late, Captain Bligh," replied Christian. Bligh and 18 others were set adrift in an open boat with provisions that included bread, pork, water and a compass.

Bligh set his course for the island of Timor in the East Indies. Although it was 3,600 miles away, it was the nearest European settlement. On the journey, he and his men avoided the other islands they sighted. Because they had no firearms, they preferred the dangers of the sea to the unfriendly natives. When they passed the Fiji Islands, natives followed them in canoes. Bligh and his crew had to row fiercely to escape them.

There were many hardships and hazards on the voyage. The men on the small boat suffered from extreme hunger. They were wet, cold, and cramped much of the time. It rained often, and they had to bail water from the boat. On the way to Timor, Bligh steered past the dangerous Great Barrier Reef off Australia. He also went through the narrow Torres Strait between Australia and New Guinea. After 41 days at sea, Bligh arrived at Timor, thus completing a lengthy and heroic open boat voyage.

Captain Bligh and his loyal men are cast adrift in a small boat by the *Bounty* mutineers.

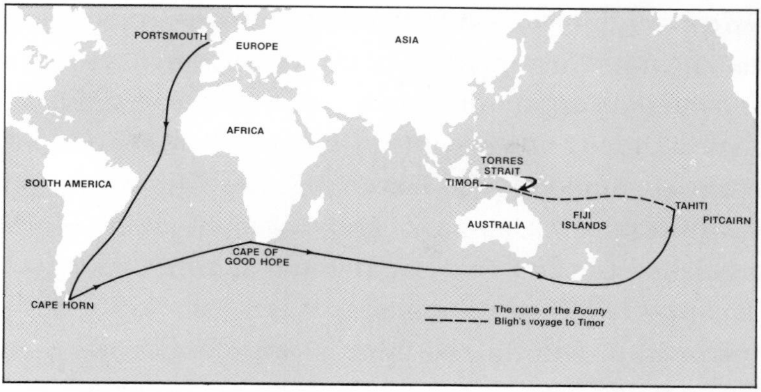

Captain Bligh and his men returned to London. There, Bligh was brought to trial for losing the *Bounty* to mutineers. He was found innocent and promoted to the rank of commander. He was also given another chance to collect and replant breadfruit in the West Indies.

As captain of the *Providence*, Bligh left again for Otaheiti. He spent two months on the island while his crew collected bredfruit trees. Then he sailed to the West Indies to transplant them. Ironically, after all of Bligh's trouble with the breadfruit, the Negro slaves in the West Indies found it tasteless and refused to eat it. To make matters worse, Bligh acquired an embarrassing nickname—"Breadfruit Bligh."

The breadfuit plant

After Bligh returned from the final breadfruit mission, he was given his first politically important naval command. He was named captain of the *Director* in a war against the Dutch. Bligh led the *Director* into battle and helped bring about the surrender of the Dutch admiral's flagship. Later, in a war against Denmark and Sweden, Bligh further distinguished himself as a capable naval commander.

In spite of his achievements, Bligh was still a subject of controversy. During the later years of his career, complaints by naval crews became common in the British navy, along with desertions and mutinies. On several occasions, Bligh was involved in serious disputes with his men. He was accused of being harsh and abusive, or too strict in enforcing navy regulations. In spite of these conflicts, Bligh was respected by his superiors.

In 1814, Bligh received his last naval promotion—Vice Admiral of the Blue. Three years later, at the age of 64, William Bligh died.

The life and career of the famous captain of the *Bounty* was thus ended. But what had been the fate of the mutineers who had played such an important role in Bligh's career? When Bligh returned to England following the mutiny on the *Bounty*, the British government sent an expedition to search for the missing mutineers. The expedition found 14 of them on Otaheiti. These mutineers were returned to England and brought to trial. Three of them were hanged. But the rest of the mutineers, Fletcher Christian, and the *Bounty* itself seemed to have disappeared. Nothing was heard of them for 18 years after the mutiny.

Bounty Bay on the island of Pitcairn

Finally, in 1808, Captain Mayhew Folger of the American trading vessel *Topaz* stumbled onto their hiding place while searching for seals. It was a small island called Pitcairn that had been incorrectly charted. Of the nine mutineers who had hidden there, Folger found only one survivor, John Adams.

Adams told Captain Folger what had happened to the missing men. He said that after the mutiny, Fletcher Christian returned to Otaheiti. He left some of the mutineers there and picked up 6 native men and 12 native women. With the natives and the 9 remaining mutineers, Christian went to the uninhabited island of Pitcairn.

Because the mutineers feared discovery, they burned the *Bounty* in what is now known as Bounty Bay, an inlet of the island. After a few years on Pitcairn, jealousy over women triggered a massacre. Among the men, only John Adams survived.

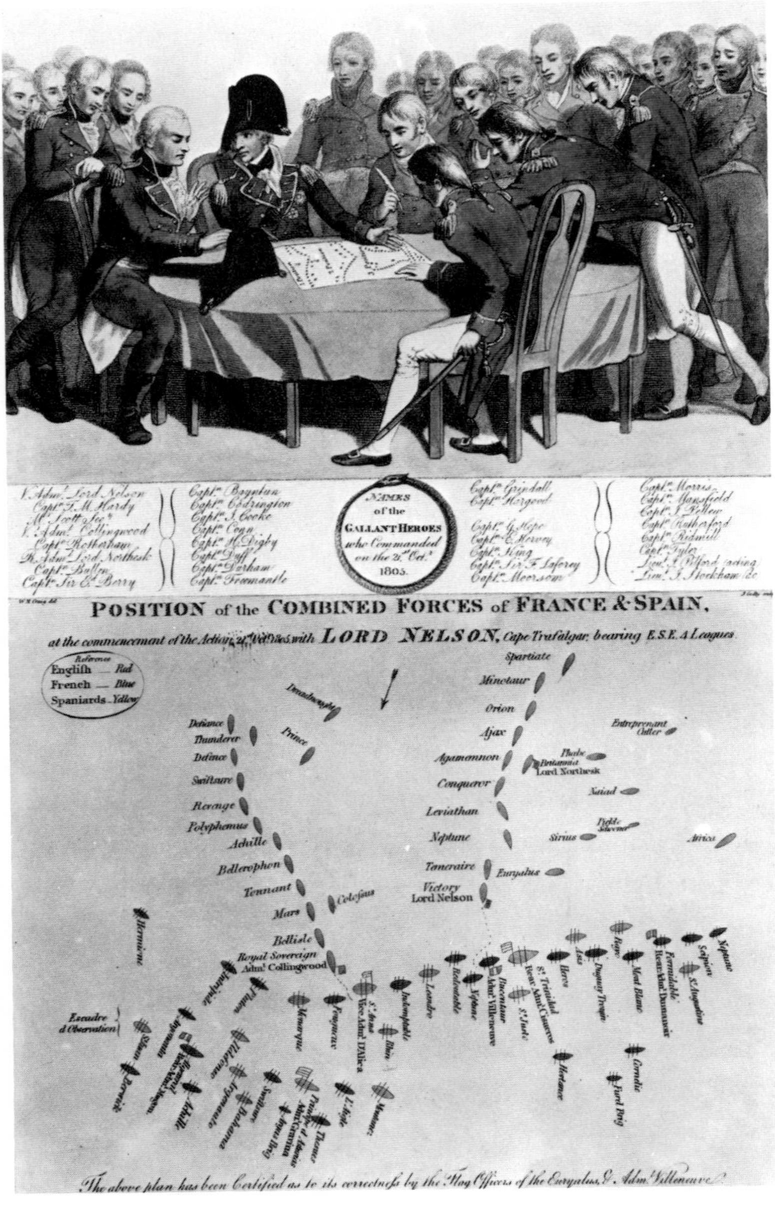
V. Adml. Lord Nelson
Captn. T. M. Hardy
Mr. Scott Secy.
V. Adml. Collingwood
Captn. Rotherham
R. Adml. Lord Northesk
Captn. Bullen
Captn. Sir Ed. Berry
Captn. Boynton
Captn. Codrington
Captn. J. Cooke
Captn. Conn
Captn. H. Digby
Captn. Duff
Captn. Durham
Captn. Freemantle
NAMES of the GALLANT HEROES who Commanded on the 21st Octr. 1805.
Captn. Grindall
Captn. Hargood
Captn. G. Hope
Captn. E. Hervey
Captn. King
Captn. Sir F. Laforey
Captn. Moorsom
Captn. Morris
Captn. Mansfield
Captn. I. Pellew
Captn. Rutherford
Captn. Redmill
Captn. Tyler
Lieut. J. Pilford acting
Lieut. J. Stockham do.
POSITION of the COMBINED FORCES of FRANCE & SPAIN,
at the commencement of the Action 21st Octr. 1805 with LORD NELSON, Cape Trafalgar bearing E.S.E. 4 Leagues
Reference
English — Red
French — Blue
Spaniards — Yellow
Spartiate
Minotaur
Orion
Ajax
Agamemnon
Britannia
Lord Northesk
Conqueror
Leviathan
Neptune
Temeraire
Victory
Lord Nelson
Entreprenant Cutter
Phœbe
Naiad
Sirius
Africa
Euryalus
Dreadnought
Prince
Defiance
Thunderer
Defence
Swiftsure
Revenge
Polyphemus
Achille
Bellerophon
Tonnant
Colossus
Mars
Bellisle
Royal Sovereign
Adml. Collingwood
Escadre d'Observation
The above plan has been Certified as to its correctness by the Flag Officers of the Euryalus, & Adml. Villeneuve.

Lord Nelson and his officers in a strategy conference. The diagram shows the positions of the ships that took part in the Battle of Trafalgar.

Lord Horatio Nelson

(1758-1805)

Horatio Nelson was England's greatest admiral and a brave and colorful naval hero. He fell in love with the sea early in life. His father was a country parson, but his uncle was a sea captain, and he encouraged young Nelson's dream of going to sea. He took the boy on a voyage to the Falkland Islands in the South Atlantic in 1770, when Nelson was only 12. Nelson joined the British navy at 15. Five years later he was named post captain and given command of his own ship. Then fate began to mold his future.

In 1793, Louis XVI of France was guillotined by revolutionaries who declared war on England. After the war broke out, Nelson was given command of the 64-gun battleship *Agamemnon.* Although Nelson was a junior officer, he showed superior leadership abilities in helping capture the French island of Corsica. During this battle, Nelson lost the sight of one eye. But his superior officer hesitated to honor the brilliant young man who outshone him.

The British fleet at anchor in calm waters

In 1797, Nelson finally gained the recognition he deserved. He was made rear admiral a week before the Battle of Cape St. Vincent in the Mediterranean. Nelson proved his ability again in this battle. In a daring move, he sailed out of the British line of ships into the enemy's path. Other British ships soon followed Nelson. As a result, the French were confused and lost the battle. The victory was a well-needed boost for England. Again, Nelson's quick thinking was not mentioned in the official naval account.

A few months later, Nelson suffered the only serious defeat of his career at Santa Cruz de Tenerife in the Canary Islands. Unable to get close to shore before daylight, the British could not surprise the enemy. And victory depended upon surprise. But Nelson insisted on fighting, even when the odds were heavily against the British. Landing on the beach at Santa Cruz, Nelson was cut down by a shot in his elbow. One of his officers found him unconscious and helped him back to his ship, where his arm was crudely amputated.

In 1798, after recovering from his wound, Nelson was given an order to find and destroy the French fleet in the Mediterranean. It was an important assignment for Nelson. With his 13 ships he played hide-and-seek with the French. When he did not find them in Egyptian waters, Nelson became discouraged and left. Then he learned that the French had merely escaped from his ships in a storm, so he returned to trap them.

Nelson held a meeting with his officers to discuss strategy. He wanted to aim his best forces at the main part of the enemy's fleet and destroy it before the other French ships were able to act. Even though it was risky, Nelson planned to attack at night. Just before sunset on August 1, 1798, the Battle of the Nile began in Aboukir Bay near Egypt. The French had not expected battle until morning and were unprepared.

After a fierce struggle, in which Nelson was again wounded, the French fleet was almost destroyed. The French army, led by Napoleon Bonaparte, was stranded in Egypt.

For his stunning defeat of the French, Nelson was hailed a national and world hero. Napoleon was forced to desert his forces and flee across the Mediterranean in a tiny ship. The French fleet never fully recovered from this blow.

Nelson then left for Naples, Italy, to recover from his new wound. There, he fell in love with Emma Hamilton, the British ambassador's wife. She became his lifelong mistress. After a year and a half in Naples, Nelson was called back to England.

In 1801, Nelson was sent to the Baltic Sea as second in command in a war against Denmark. The British government had decided to attack the Danish fleet because it had been smuggling for the French. Nelson knew that bold action was needed and took matters into his own hands. He convinced his commander that they should attack the Danes in Copenhagen quickly. In the midst of the ensuing battle, Nelson's commander, fearing defeat, gave a signal to stop the action. Nelson put a telescope to his blind eye and pretended not to see the signal. Nelson's bravery was rewarded, for in an hour the Danes surrendered. Nelson was then formally honored by the British and was granted a title.

Following the war against the Danes, Nelson lived quietly at his country home in England with Emma Hamilton for two years. Then in 1803, war with France was resumed and Nelson was named commander-in-chief of the British fleet. Nelson again went to sea to locate and destroy the French.

Lord Nelson falls, mortally wounded, on the deck of the *Victory*.

When an attempt to trap the French in the West Indies proved unsuccessful, Nelson turned his attention to the Mediterranean. After a long sea search he discovered that his ships were only 24 hours behind the French fleet. The final battle was at hand.

The Battle of Trafalgar began on October 21, 1805. Nelson predicted that he would die and seemed unconcerned about his safety. He insisted on wearing his striking commander's jacket and, for the first time, did not carry a sword. Nelson also insisted on leading the charge in his own flagship, the *Victory*, and would not transfer to another ship.

As the *Victory* drew closer to the French ships, she began to suffer from the beating being given to her. Soon the *Victory* was grinding sides with the French *Redoutable*. Unknown to Nelson, the *Redoutable's* captain excelled in close action. Shots flew through the sails of the *Victory*, and they were soon in shreds. One of the masts came crashing down. The wheel was shot away, and the ship could barely be steered. Many of Nelson's men were slaughtered on the deck. Nelson had found the close combat he wanted. He walked the quarterdeck through the gun smoke. Suddenly, he was hit.

"They have come for me at last," Nelson gasped. "My backbone is shot through."

As he was carried below the deck, he covered his face with a handkerchief so that his men would not become discouraged. Nelson remained conscious for two hours before he died, and he demanded news of the battle in spite of his suffering.

Nelson's death came at a moment of victory for the British. Although outnumbered, the British had defeated the French. Napoleon's idea of invading England by sea was forgotten as he directed his energies to the rest of Europe.

The Battle of Trafalgar was considered a turning point in modern British history. It established Great Britain's rule of the seas for the rest of the 19th century. The battle also secured Nelson's place in history. His personality inspired imagination and boldness in his officers, and he has remained a model for generations of British sailors. A famous statue of Lord Nelson now stands in Trafalgar Square in London.

Joshua Slocum

(1844-1909?)

The sea has a special lure for some men. Those who dare to probe its mysteries and challenge its moods are perhaps not understood by their brothers on land. Most people want the comfort and security that a home on land provides. And they do not want to be alone. Joshua Slocum was a man who had the courage to face the challenge of the sea by himself.

Slocum was born in 1844 on a farm in the sea-swept province of Nova Scotia in Canada. His love for the surrounding ocean was greater than his loyalty to the family farm. At 14 he ran away from home and signed on as a cook on a fishing schooner.

Joshua Slocum aboard his ship, *Spray*, in a South American port, 1895

This job began Slocum's career at sea. He traveled widely on trading vessels in the South Pacific and the Orient. Eventually, he became captain of his own commercial ship, the *Aquidneck*. This ship carried cargoes to South America and the West Indies. When the *Aquidneck* ran aground and was destroyed, Slocum was left without funds and without a ship. In 1886, when this disaster occurred, steamships had replaced sailing vessels. As a result, Slocum was unable to get command of another ship. It seemed as though he was fated to live out his days far from his beloved oceans.

Then a whaling captain offered Slocum an old ship, the *Spray*. Slocum repaired the vessel carefully. He decided to sail the 37-foot sloop around the world alone. He was then 51 years old, and, in a way, he had been preparing for this journey throughout his life. In April 1895, the *Spray* was ready to leave. Slocum sailed her out of Boston harbor and headed across the Atlantic.

Slocum's plan was to sail eastward to the Mediterranean Sea. He was forced off his course, however, by some pirates. As the pirates chased the *Spray*, Slocum prepared for a gun battle. Then fortune stepped in on his side. A huge wave broke the mast of the pirate ship and the chase ended. But Slocum was no longer headed for the Mediterranean. He was sailing towards South American waters.

On the way, Slocum made friends with a wounded dolphin by giving it scraps of food. It followed him for 1,000 miles. Sharks also followed Slocum on his journey. He learned that if he threw a tin plate into the water, the sharks would rise to snatch it, thinking it was food. When they surfaced, Slocum shot them in the head.

Sharks were but a minor worry for Slocum. When he reached the Straits of Magellan at the southern tip of South America, he had great difficulty steering his ship through the stormy waters. Again and again he tried to push the *Spray* into the Pacific. But he was forced back into the waters surrounding the island of Tierra del Fuego. There he was to face some very dangerous opponents. Some of the natives on the island were no better than bandits.

The leader of these cutthroats, Black Pedro, followed Slocum's ship and wanted to board it. To make Black Pedro and his men think that he was not alone, Slocum went down into his cabin several times and changed clothes. Then he fired a shot at the natives. They finally stopped chasing him, but it had been a close call.

Again, Slocum tried to enter the Pacific. Storms with tremendous winds pushed the *Spray* off course and stripped her of her sails. Only the bare masts were left. Slocum could do nothing but let the wind direct the boat. The strong wind brought hail and sleet which cut Slocom's face. Unable to navigate, he came dangerously close to crashing on the rocks. But luck was on Slocum's side again—he succeeded in escaping the rocks and reached calm waters.

Slocum trapped in a difficult situation. He must frighten away the fierce natives of Tierra del Fuego.

Slocum was then followed by another group of hostile natives. One night, before he went to sleep in the cabin, he spread carpet tacks over the deck. At midnight he was awakened by the screams and howls of the natives who had come aboard and stepped on the tacks. As they jumped overboard, Slocum fired at them to make sure they didn't return. But the natives were still a danger. Their canoes carried torches which could be thrown on board. Slocum finally met with them and bribed their leader with the gift of a knife, promising more presents on the following day. But Slocum sailed from their territory that night.

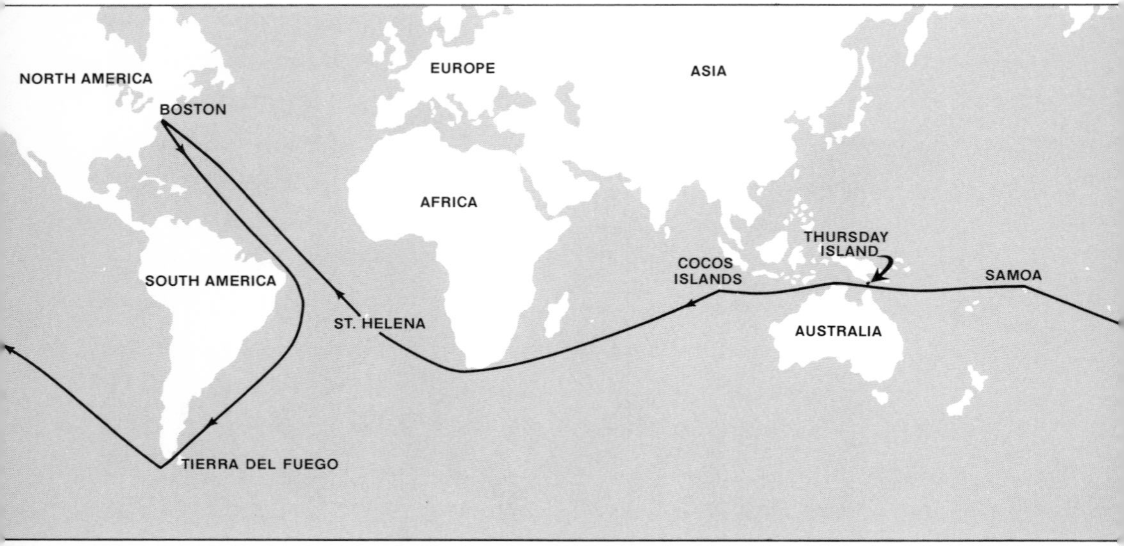

Slocum's route around the world

Finally, the open sea lay ahead. Slocum set his course for the Samoan Islands in the South Pacific. His only companions on this leg of the journey were flying fish, which he sometimes caught and ate. Slocum's potatoes, which were his favorite food, became rotten before he could again reach land. His diet and his days became tedious. After two and a half months, he reached Samoa.

Slocum took on supplies in Samoa and set out again, this time for Australia. When he reached Australia, he met with disappointment. Official yacht clubs refused to acknowledge his voyage because he had not registered his ship and course properly before leaving Boston. Undaunted, however, he sailed from Thursday Island north of Australia.

Slocum's destination was the Cocos Islands in the Indian Ocean. This proved to be the smoothest leg of his journey. He sailed 2,700 miles in 23 days. He had set his course so perfectly, and the winds and currents had been so favorable, that he had had to steer his ship for only three hours of the 23 days.

After reaching the Cocos Islands and again taking on supplies, Slocum began the last part of his journey. From the Indian Ocean, he sailed to South Africa, around the Cape of Good Hope, and into the South Atlantic. At the island of St. Helena, the governor gave Slocum a goat as a companion on the *Spray*. The goat promptly ate Slocum's map of the West Indies and his straw hat. Slocum left the goat behind at the next island he stopped at. The only animals that Slocum could get along with were the spiders that had come with him from Boston.

The sturdy *Spray*, with its daring captain at the helm

In June 1898, Slocum sailed home to Boston in the *Spray*, becoming the first person to sail around the world alone. He had sailed 46,000 miles in three years.

When Slocum arrived in Boston, he did not receive the welcome he had expected. The newspapers and the public were concerned with the Spanish-American War and did not give him much publicity. In fact, he had to prove to some doubters that his voyage was not a fake. He soon gained the fame he deserved, however, when he wrote *Sailing Around the World Alone*, which became a best seller.

Slocum lectured and tried farming. But he was restless, and the sea beckoned. In 1909, at the age of 65, he sailed off alone for South America. He was never heard from again.

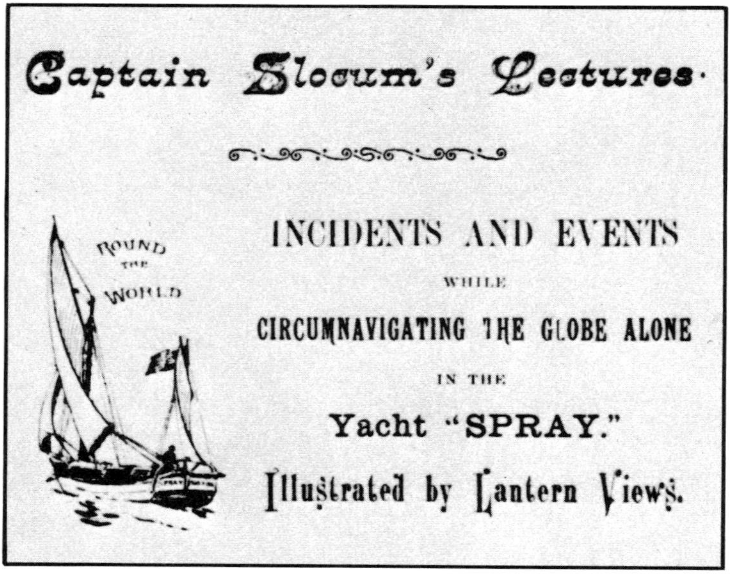

Ernest Shackleton (second from left) and three sea-weary crew members

Ernest Shackleton

(1875-1922)

In 1891, at the age of 16, Ernest Shackleton left school and a comfortable middle-class life for the cramped quarters of a British sailing ship. As a member of the British merchant marine and later the British navy, he traveled the world's oceans for 10 more years. Shackleton was intelligent and trustworthy, and eventually he became an officer.

In 1901, Shackleton was chosen to go on Robert F. Scott's Antarctic expedition aboard the ship *Discovery*. Since he was a junior officer, Shackleton felt honored. He developed symtoms of scurvy, however, during the first winter of the expedition. Although he endured his sickness heroically, Shackleton was sent home when the season ended. His bravery and skill had not been questioned by his leaders, but his pride was hurt.

Shackleton could not forget the South Pole and was determined to prove that he was fit for polar exploration. Shackleton wanted to lead his own expedition. But he felt he was a rival of his friend and former leader, Robert Scott. Finally, they managed to work out an agreement. Shackleton consented to explore only areas where Scott had not been.

Shackleton set sail in the *Nimrod* and reached Antarctica in 1907. He traveled farther south than Scott had, but because of a shortage of food, he and his three companions did not reach the South Pole. They were lucky, in fact, to be able to return home. Shackleton was disappointed, but he became a popular hero. He wrote a book about his experiences called *Heart of the Antarctic.*

When Shackleton was 40 years old, he organized another expedition aimed at the South Pole. In 1914, he and a 28-man crew left England in the *Endurance.* They stopped at the remote island of South Georgia before starting the final voyage to the Antarctic Circle. Shackleton's goal was to cross the Antarctic ice cap and reach the South Pole.

In January 1915, the *Endurance* became trapped by ice in the dangerous Weddell Sea. It was crushed by the massive pieces of ice and had to be abandoned. Shackleton's mission was doomed, and he and his men were castaways on the ice pack surrounding Antarctica.

The *Endurance*, wrecked and trapped by ice

There was no hope of rescue. The crew's only goal was to stay alive. No one else knew where they were or that they were in trouble. The men and their dogs hauled tents, three small boats, and supplies over the endless ice in search of a water route to freedom.

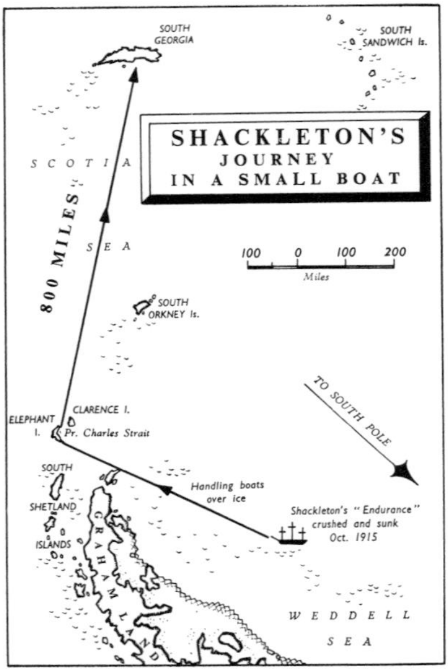

Shackleton's journey
in the whaleboat

"Waiting, waiting, waiting," one man wrote in his diary, describing the dull daily routine of camp life. They all hoped to find open water on which they could sail to reach civilization. For six months, they waited for a gap to appear in the ice.

Finally, the ice began to crumble. But Shackleton and his men could not launch their boats because the vessels would have been smashed into pieces by the moving icebergs. Then, just when their situation seemed hopeless, an opening appeared.

"Launch the boats!" Shackleton shouted. The three small boats which had been saved from the wrecked *Endurance* were loaded with supplies and the men boarded them. The boats were turned homeward.

On the return voyage, high waves rolled over the boats and soaked the men. They had to keep wiggling their toes to keep them from freezing. The icy water was sometimes knee deep. Ice formed on the boats and had to be chopped off. The men were miserable and suffered from thirst, salt-water boils, and white rings of frostbite. They were kept busy bailing, and they thought that at any moment their journey would end tragically.

The expedition crossed the easternmost end of the dreaded Drake Passage below South America, and the men saw its legendary cliff-high waves, which were called "gray-beards." Somehow they survived this stormiest part of all the oceans. But their greatest enemy was ice. If the ice hit them at night, they would be crushed.

Finally, when the expedition had gone three and a half days without food or water, Elephant Island was sighted. When they reached it, they found it uninhabited and barren. After resting there, Shackleton decided to leave the main part of his group on Elephant Island. He and five men would try to reach the island of South Georgia 800 miles to the north.

Although it was small and half rotten, a 22-foot whale-boat was chosen for the trip. The deck was covered with canvas to keep the inside dry.

The whaleboat approaches the island of South Georgia through treacherous waters.

Once underway, the rescue party faced more discomfort and danger. Water seeped into the boat continuously, and the men were always wet. Their knees were raw from crawling over the rocks that had been loaded into the bottom of the boat to make it heavier. They were very cramped and cold. Two sleeping bags had to be thrown overboard because they were waterlogged and slimy. The sleeping bags had been stuffed with reindeer hair and wet clumps of it were on the men's faces and hands and in their food.

When Shackleton's estimates showed that they were halfway to South Georgia, the men became more cheerful. After 14 days, some seaweed and a bird were sighted, which meant that land was nearby. But it was very foggy and the men worried about missing the island and being forever doomed to the endless ocean beyond. There was also another possibility—they could smash into the island's high cliffs.

"Land!" cried one of the men, sighting South Georgia.

"We've done it," Shackleton said, confident that he had finally led his men to safety. But he was wrong. The weather suddenly changed, and it seemed certain that high winds would drive their weak boat against the rocks. Exhausted, the men struggled bravely against the storm while sea water poured into their boat. Again, all seemed lost.

But Shackleton guided his small boat carefully through the waves and dangerous, hidden reefs to the shore. They landed at last. In a short time, they were drinking from a fresh stream of water.

The rescue mission was not finished, however. The men had to reach the whaling station on the other side of the island. Shackleton decided that he and two others would travel overland across unexplored wilderness and mountains.

After a hazardous two-day journey, the three men approached the whaling station which they had left nearly a year and a half before. Walking up to the manager of the station, one of the weary men simply said, "My name is Shackleton."

The men on the other side of South Georgia were rescued on the next day. Shackleton and a rescue party made four attempts to save the men still marooned on Elephant Island before they finally reached them. It had been four months since Shackleton had left, and the lonely survivors had given up hope.

In spite of the suffering he and his men had endured, Shackleton could never forget the challenge of Antarctica. In 1922, he left England on the *Quest* to lead a third expedition. While off the coast of South Georgia, Shackleton died suddenly of a heart attack. He is buried on the island.

The survivors on Elephant Island greet their rescuers.

Lieutenant John F. Kennedy

(1917-1963)

Most people remember John Kennedy as a young energetic American president. When he was assassinated in Dallas on November 22, 1963, the nation mourned his cruel, early death. Kennedy knew that he was risking his life by riding in an open car that day, but he had always been a man who confronted danger courageously. During World War II, when he was only 26 years old, he survived an adventure at sea in which his endurance and courage were severely tested.

Blackett Strait

A lieutenant in the navy, Kennedy was stationed in the South Pacific during the war. He served as captain of PT 109, a small craft armed with torpedos. On August 2, 1943, Kennedy's boat and 15 other PT boats were sent to patrol the Blackett Strait in the Solomon Islands.

On that same night, four Japanese destroyers had secretly sailed through the Blackett Strait. One of the destroyers, the *Amagiri*, carried barges and supplies which were unloaded at a secret landing. Then the ship began to return through the Strait. At the same time, Kennedy, in PT 109, was searching for other American ships in the waters of the Strait.

"Ship ahead!" yelled one of Kennedy's crew. The dark, blurry shape looked like a PT boat—but just for an instant. It soon became apparent that a Japanese destroyer was coming toward them at high speed. It was the *Amagiri.*

The *Amagiri* split PT 109 in half. Chaos followed. The gasoline tanks set the stern, or rear of the boat, ablaze. Kennedy was thrown on his back against the cockpit and then onto the deck. Fearing an explosion, he quickly jumped overboard. As the fire died down and the stern sank, Kennedy swam to the bow, or front, of PT 109. He called to his crew and found most of them drifting in the darkness with their safety vests on. After spending hours in the water searching for his men, Kennedy found 10 survivors. One man had severe burns on his body. Another was vomiting and partly unconscious from gasoline fumes. Two men were missing.

Kennedy and his men clung to the bow of the disabled boat until daylight finally came. Since the Japanese controlled the nearby islands, the crew worried that they might be spotted. Also, the boat could sink at any time. The shipwrecked men could wait no longer to be rescued by a PT boat.

Kennedy decided, therefore, that they would swim to nearby Plum Pudding Island before dark. He told the others to hold on to a plank of wood so that they wouldn't get separated. Kennedy put the strap of the burned man's life jacket in his teeth. Four hours later, the crew reached the island after a long and tiring swim. Kennedy collapsed on shore with his burden, exhausted and vomiting salt water. He had towed the injured sailor for nearly four miles.

The marooned men did not explore the island because they feared that the Japanese were on it. But Kennedy felt that some action was necessary. Against the advice of his men, he swam out into the sea that night to locate PT boats that might be cruising by. Kennedy took a lantern which floated on a life preserver, and carried a loaded pistol tied on a rope around his neck. He thought that loud shots and a bright light would attract the attention of the PT boats.

It was a tiring swim and Kennedy tried not to think of sharks. He waited for PT boats, but saw none. Then, as he tried to swim back to the island, a strong current carried him off course. He was washed ashore on another island, where he collapsed and slept until morning. At dawn, he saw where he was and swam back to his men. They had nearly given up hope that he would return. The next night another man swam out into the sea as Kennedy had done, but no PT boats passed.

Kennedy (far right) and the crew of PT 109

PT boats are fast and effective in close-to-shore skirmishes.

Realizing that no one knew where they were, Kennedy thought that he and his men should swim to another island. They left Plum Pudding Island and swam to Olasana Island. On Olasana, they could see a United States base, Rendova Harbor, which was 38 miles away. But they had no way to reach Rendova Harbor.

At last, friendly natives helped Kennedy to escape from Olasana. They put him in the bottom of their canoe and covered him with palms so that the Japanese could not see him. As they crossed the sea passage to safety, Japanese planes circled overhead. One of the natives stood up and waved at the Japanese to show that they were not enemies. Kennedy arrived safely at Rendova Harbor on August 7, 1943, and guided a PT boat back to Olasana to pick up his men.

For his heroism and leadership in this action, Kennedy received the Navy and Marine Corps Medal. He also received a Purple Heart for the injury to his back. But Kennedy's health had been severely weakened. He was returned to the United States to recover. After he regained his health, he entered political life. Politics was a new type of adventure, and, as history shows, Kennedy was prepared for it.

Heyerdahl's raft, *Kon-Tiki*, at sea

Thor Heyerdahl

(1914-)

Thor Heyerdahl (toor HI-ur-doll) became a famous sea captain almost by accident. His real purpose in going to sea was to prove a scientific theory. Heyerdahl had been interested in science throughout his childhood in Larvik, Norway. His parents were enthusiastic about the outdoors and the history of primitive people, and their young son caught the scientific fever at an early age. This proved to be an important influence in Heyerdahl's choice of a career.

The Indian rafts of ancient Peru. Heyerdahl modeled the *Kon-Tiki* after these rafts.

As a young man, Heyerdahl studied zoology and geography at the University of Oslo. Then in 1937, he and his young bride went to live for a year on Fatu-Hiva, an island in the South Pacific. They went there to study the animals and to search for a better and more primitive way of life. It was on Fatu-Hiva that Heyerdahl first learned of Tiki, the legendary father of the Polynesian people. He also learned that there were fair-skinned natives on some of the Polynesian islands.

After a year of work and study on Fatu-Hiva, Heyerdahl returned to Norway. But the memory of Tiki and the mystery of the origins of the fair-skinned people haunted him. He began to work on a theory.

Heyerdahl learned that South American Indian legends told of an ancient god-like race of people. The legends said that these people were tall and fair-skinned and had lived in South America before the Inca Indians. Most of these people had been massacred in a battle in the Andes Mountains. But their leader, Kon-Tiki, and some companions had escaped to the Pacific coast. Heyerdahl believed that they had sailed on balsa wood rafts to Polynesia and settled there. Heyerdahl wanted to make such a voyage himself. He felt that if he succeeded in reaching Polynesia, he could show that Kon-Tiki might have made the voyage in earlier times. Kon-Tiki's voyage would, in turn, account for the presence of fair-skinned natives on the Polynesian Islands.

Scientists were very doubtful about Heyerdahl's theory. Most of them believed that the natives of Polynesia had come from Asia. Financial backers hesitated to loan him money because they seriously doubted that he would survive the trip. However, after many difficulties, Heyerdahl received the money he needed. He was ready to begin preparations for the voyage from South America to the South Pacific.

Heyerdahl's first step was to build the balsa wood raft. He needed fresh balsa logs, with the sap still in them, so that the raft would not become soaked with water and sink. In order to get nine fresh balsa logs, Heyerdahl had to go into the jungles of Ecuador and chop down his own trees. He and his men constructed the raft in the same way the Indians had. No nails or wire rope were used. The raft was christened *Kon-Tiki*, after the legendary pre-Inca king.

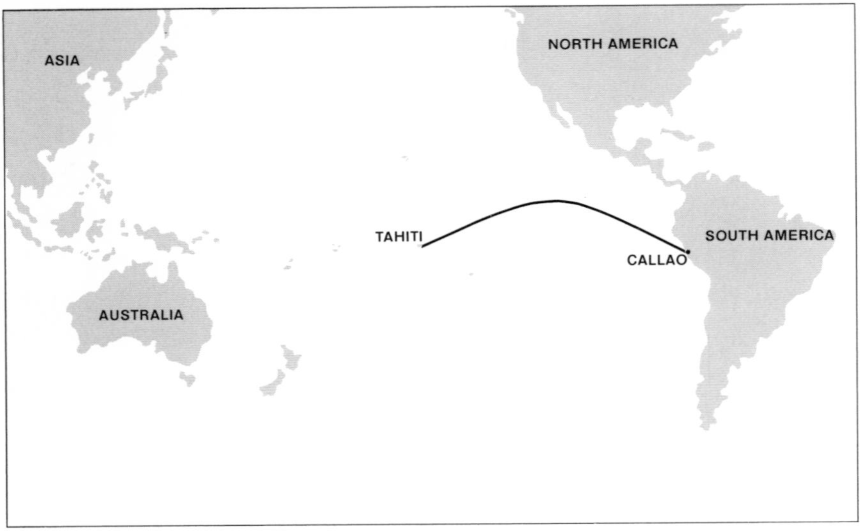

The route of the *Kon-Tiki*

The *Kon-Tiki*, with its six-man Norwegian crew, was towed out of Callao Bay in Peru and left 50 miles from land. Heyerdahl hoped that the Humboldt current off the coast of South America would carry the raft westward. It did, and the *Kon-Tiki* sailed into the open Pacific.

The voyage was both exciting and dangerous. The crew became immediately fascinated with the many kinds of sea creatures, especially the dolphins. At least six of them followed the raft daily. Fish landed on the raft frequently, and it was the cook's first duty in the morning to collect them. One night a member of the crew, who was sleeping on deck, was awakened by something cold and wet flapping by his ears. It was a snake mackerel, a rare deep-sea fish with long, sharp teeth. He quickly returned it to the water.

Thor Heyerdahl (left) and a crew member with a lucky catch

Other sea creatures proved to be more of a threat. One time a whale shark 50 feet long and weighing 15 tons circled the raft for about an hour. It could easily have smashed the *Kon-Tiki*. Finally, one of the crew thrust an eight-foot harpoon into the whale shark's head. The harpoon line snapped and the huge fish dove into the depths. It never returned.

Another crisis occurred when a crewman fell into the ocean while trying to retrieve a sleeping bag. The crew could barely hear his cries above the noise of the waves. The raft was unable to stop or turn around and pick him up. A lifebelt was thrown to him, but the wind blew it back. Then a crewman jumped into the water with a lifebelt and rope and was able to pull the man to safety.

Storms were also a problem. One storm lasted five days and seriously weakened the raft. The ropes which bound the *Kon-Tiki* together had worn their way into the logs. If modern wire ropes had been used, the logs would have been cut into pieces.

In spite of the dangers, Heyerdahl and his crew still found time for amusement. They built a bamboo basket that looked like a cage and lowered it below the raft to collect and observe fish and other forms of sea life. The crew also rowed in a small rubber boat called a dinghy. A rope from the raft was connected to the dinghy so that it would not drift away. The cabin offered the most pleasure for the crew. It was there they found shelter and privacy. All of them read there and one played the guitar for his shipmates.

Heyerdahl at the helm of the *Kon-Tiki*

After 101 days at sea, the raft approached an island. But the crew could not land the *Kon-Tiki* because the island had a sharp, jagged coral reef surrounding it. Helplessly, they were swept sideways toward the reef.

The *Kon-Tiki* rode the crest of a high wave over the reef and thus avoided a disaster, but the raft was considerably damaged. Leaving the raft on the reef, the crew waded through the shallow waters to shore. The island was one of a group of islands near Tahiti. Heyerdahl and his men had sailed 4,300 miles and had successfully reached Polynesia.

Heyerdahl wrote about the voyage in his famous book *Kon-Tiki.* He had proved that his theory about Indian migrations across the South Pacific was possible. Therefore, he finally attained a respectable position in the scientific community.

The *Ra II* in the harbor at Safi, Morocco, before the transatlantic voyage

Twenty-two years after the voyage of the *Kon-Tiki*, Heyerdahl turned his attention to the Atlantic Ocean. He wanted to prove that Egyptians had reached the Yucatan Peninsula in Mexico 3,000 years before Columbus arrived. Heyerdahl believed that the Egyptians had traveled in papyrus reed boats, so again he constructed a similar craft. He named his new boat after the Egyptian sun-god Ra. Heyerdahl left Safi, Morocco, in July 1969. But heavy seas forced him and his crew to abandon the *Ra* 600 miles from Barbados in the West Indies.

Refusing to admit failure, Heyerdahl built *Ra II*, a shorter, lighter, and stronger boat. He and an international crew started again from Safi in May 1970. This time they succeeded, reaching Barbados after a 3,200-mile voyage that lasted 57 days. Messages of congratulations for Heyerdahl poured into Barbados from around the world.

Heyerdahl has received many honors from many different countries. As a scientist, explorer, and sea captain, he has won worldwide popularity. Heyerdahl's two famous vessels, the *Kon-Tiki* and the *Ra II*, are kept in the Kon-Tiki Museum in Oslo, Norway.

In 1971 Thor Heyerdahl testified before a U.S. Senate subcommittee investigating air and ocean pollution. He reported that the *Ra II* had sailed through floating globs of oil and other debris for 43 of the 57 days that the boat was at sea.

Jacques-Yves Cousteau

(1910-   )

Jacques-Yves Cousteau (zjak-eev koo-STOW) is a modern pioneer in an area that man has traditionally avoided—the underwater world. Underwater exploration had been impossible until the 20th century. Explorers needed equipment to help them move about in a watery environment. Cousteau has helped to erase ignorance about the sea by inventing devices which enable men to work and even live under the water, and by exploring the sea floor himself.

When Cousteau was a young student in France's naval academy, his arm was paralyzed in an automobile accident. But he refused to accept his handicap. To regain strength in the injured arm, Cousteau began swimming in the Mediterranean. He was successful, and the use of his arm was restored. Then, in 1936, when Cousteau was 26 years old, a fellow naval officer gave him a pair of goggles which had been used by a pearl fisherman. Diving with goggles opened exciting new possibilities for Cousteau, and it led to his lifelong interest in underwater life.

World War II interrupted Cousteau's diving in the Mediterranean. He served in the French navy and later in the French Underground. In 1943, he helped to develop the aqua-lung, which enabled divers to carry air with them underwater to depths of 300 feet. After the war, he used the aqua-lung to search for mines off the Mediterranean coast.

With the invention of the aqua-lung, Cousteau was launched on his career as an undersea explorer. He was recognized as a leader in the exciting new science of oceanography, or study of ocean life and geography. In 1951, with the financial backing of the French government, Cousteau became captain of his own research ship, the *Calypso*. He used the ship as a base for diving and exploration.

A diver using an early aqua-lung and a scooter which propels him through the water.

Cousteau did his first major work in the Mediterranean off the coast of France. At that time, he was especially interested in sea wrecks. In 1952 he learned about some buried pots which had been found accidentally by commercial divers in a lobster fishery. Cousteau suspected that the pots were ancient wine jars from a shipwreck. He decided to dive near the island of Grande Congloué near France to search for other relics.

Cousteau explored the area at a depth of 220 feet and did not find any further evidence of the shipwreck. Finally, as he was returning to the surface from a deep dive, Cousteau saw the sunken ship. It lay on a slope at a depth of 140 feet. This time he could not stay long because his oxygen supply was running low. He gathered some wine cups and an old bronze boat hook and quickly surfaced. After examining these samples, a scientist on the *Calypso* said that the ship was possibly the oldest seagoing cargo ship ever found. It was thought to be 2,200 years old.

Cousteau and his crew immediately began to try to recover the wreck. Since the water pressure was extreme, aqua-lung divers could work only several 17-minute shifts a day. Cousteau decided to use a long suction hose from the *Calypso* which would act like a vacuum cleaner to suck up mud and debris from the wreck. The crew found more wine jars in the wreckage. Some of them had broken dishes, shells, and silt at the openings. These jars had been the homes of octopuses. The animals had pulled the debris into the jars as protection from intruders.

A diver from the *Calypso* salvages wine jars from the ancient shipwreck off Grand Congloué Island.

Cousteau and his crew worked at recovering the wreckage for two years. They made 8,000 dives to bring up the remains of the ship. Finally, Cousteau and his fellow scientists were able to suggest a possible solution to the mystery of the shipwreck. The ship was probably owned by a Roman trader. In approximately 230 B.C., the ship had sailed from the Greek island of Delos. It was bound for Massalia, a Greek colony in France. The ship had been overloaded with wine and pottery. It was thought that perhaps the crew had gotten drunk on the wine and had run into the rocks just a few miles from their destination. No remains of the crew were found.

As Cousteau learned more about the possible uses of his equipment, he turned his attention from shipwrecks to deep-sea exploration. In 1956 Cousteau decided to anchor the *Calypso* in the Romanche Trench, a 25,000-foot canyon in the mid-Atlantic. The exact location of the trench was discovered by means of a depth recorder, a device which uses sound waves to indicate the depth of a particular spot on the ocean floor. When the trench was located, an anchor with a lightweight nylon cord was lowered over the side of the *Calypso*. The anchor stuck fast at a depth of four and one-half miles!

The *Denise*, an underwater diving saucer invented by Cousteau

Then Cousteau lowered a special underwater camera on another line. It took 800 pictures with an electronic flash. The pictures that were developed did not show anything as exciting as sea monsters, but they did show beautiful starfish as well as many other signs of small animal life. Cousteau and his crew charted the entire trench and left with the mission completed.

Cousteau went on many other mapping missions, and he became an expert on ocean geography. But he needed a vehicle which he could use to explore the ocean at great depths. In 1959 Cousteau invented and used the first diving saucer, the *Denise*, which was like a small submarine. It could move as freely as a diver, but it could go much deeper. Two water jets on its sides controlled its direction. It also had a mechanical arm which could be lowered to pick up objects from the sea floor.

Early tests of the *Denise* in the mid-Atlantic proved that it was seaworthy, but that it needed some adjustments. When these were made, the *Denise* was taken to the island of Corsica in the Mediterranean. There, Cousteau decided to test the craft at its maximum depth—1,000 feet. Cousteau and a crew member entered the saucer. They lay down on foam mattresses and peered out of its two portholes. The portholes looked like eyes and gave the *Denise* a slightly owlish appearance.

The *Denise* was lowered on a cable from the *Calypso*. When it was deep in the water, it was unhooked and freed. The small submarine functioned perfectly. It touched bottom at 1,000 feet and skimmed along the ocean floor. Then it surfaced without difficulty, passing upward along the side of a huge ocean cliff. The *Denise* proved to be very valuable in oceanographic research. Later, Cousteau built another sea saucer which could descend to 3,000 feet.

In recent years, Cousteau has made the undersea world more familiar to millions of people. Through the use of underwater movie cameras, many of the mysteries of the ocean have been photographed and televised. Several of these broadcasts have concerned one of Cousteau's major interests—proving that man can live and work beneath the sea. Cousteau has constructed sea houses which are independent of surface supports. The houses have kitchens, air conditioning, and communications systems which enable the men who test them and live in them to remain under the ocean for months.

The National Geographic Society medal
awarded to Cousteau in 1961

Because of this kind of vision and talent for invention, Cousteau has won worldwide fame and respect. In 1961 President John Kennedy presented Cousteau with a National Geographic Society Gold Medal. He called Cousteau "one of the great explorers of an entirely new dimension . . . having opened the ocean floor to man and to science."

Commander William R. Anderson

(1921-   )

The atomic powered submarine was developed after World War II. The United States was particularly interested in using atomic submarines to find a route under the ice cap at the North Pole. In 1957 Commander William R. Anderson of the United States Navy was named captain of the first nuclear submarine to make the underwater crossing.

This voyage under the polar ice was an important undertaking for Anderson. He was only 36 years old in 1957, when the journey began, and he was well suited for the task. Commander Anderson was a graduate of Annapolis Naval Academy and had served aboard submarines in World War II and in the Korean War. He enjoyed submarine duty. He said: "In the big-ship navy you had all that spit and polish. I got my teeth into real responsibility quicker in a sub."

Anderson found responsibility and adventure with his new command. He was given charge of the nuclear submarine *Nautilus*. Nuclear power enabled the *Nautilus* to stay submerged for long periods of time, which made it the perfect ship for sub-polar exploration. But even with all of its power and advanced guidance systems, the *Nautilus* could not operate successfully on its mission without a brave and skillful commander.

In August 1957, Anderson started on his first voyage to the Arctic by sailing into the Greenland Sea on the eastern side of the Arctic Circle. Once under the ice, Anderson had to use all of his skills as a submarine commander. His first difficulty involved damaged equipment.

The damage occurred when Anderson ordered the *Nautilus* to surface. He thought that there was a hole in the roof of ice above the submarine, but he was mistaken. When Anderson looked into both of his periscopes, he saw only blackness. The ship had run into a floating piece of thin ice which had disabled the instruments. One periscope was ruined, but the other could be fixed. The *Nautilus* surfaced, and repairs were made on the periscope in the bitter wind and cold on top of the ship. Soon, the submarine was again on its way north.

But the *Nautilus* had further trouble. There was a power failure on the master compass. Power was restored, but the crew could not be sure that the compass was operating accurately. It was possible that the *Nautilus* could circle the North Pole and the crew would not know it. Anderson decided that the risk was too great and gave the order to turn back.

Although it did not reach the Pole, the *Nautilus* had traveled farther north than any other ship. It had been submerged under the ice for 74 hours and had covered a distance of 1,000 miles. Anderson's journey was very much like a science fiction story by Jules Verne. In his book *20,000 Leagues Under the Sea*, Verne had written about a fictional *Nautilus* that had journeyed under the Polar ice.

In June 1958, Anderson and the *Nautilus* made another attempt at finding a route beneath the North Pole. This time Anderson entered the Arctic Circle from the west, through the Bering Strait between Russia and Alaska. Once beyond the strait, the *Nautilus* entered the

The *Nautilus* at anchor in Hawaii before its departure for the voyage under the polar ice

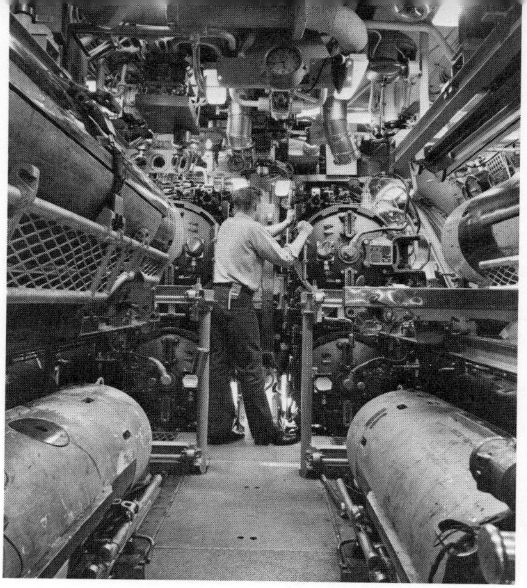

The torpedo room of the *Nautilus*. The torpedos could have been used to blast the submarine free if it had become trapped by ice.

shallow Chukchi Sea and submerged. At first, the ship's instruments indicated that the water was 160 feet deep and that the ceiling of ice was thin and would not endanger the *Nautilus* from above. Soon, however, sonar devices warned of danger. The high frequency sound waves sent out by the sonar indicated the presence of ice extending down more than 60 feet into the water. The submarine was barely able to pass beneath it.

Realizing the danger, Commander Anderson decided to turn back. He ordered the crew to take the *Nautilus* down to the point where it would lie just 20 feet from the ocean bottom. Then he ordered his men to turn it around. When the submarine was turning, sonar indicated an ice ridge ahead of the *Nautilus* that was two miles long. The submarine passed under the ridge and cleared it by only a few feet. Anderson had again failed to travel under the pole, and the *Nautilus* cruised back to Hawaii.

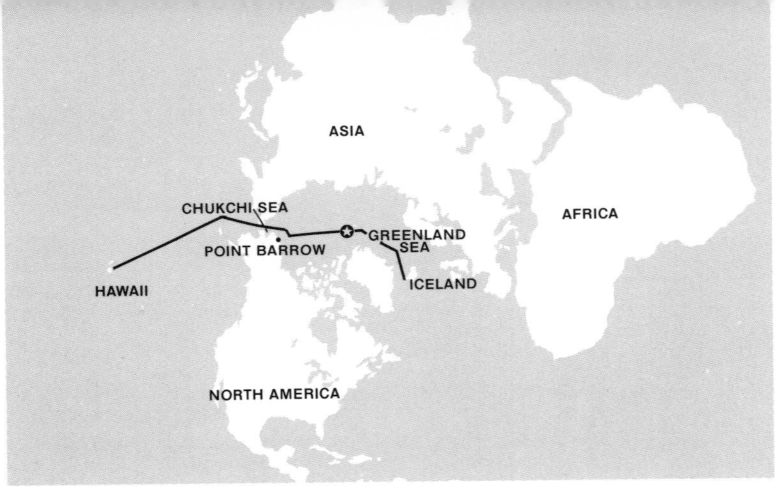

The next month the *Nautilus* was made ready once more to face the Arctic perils. On July 29, Anderson and his 116-man crew crossed the outward boundary of the Arctic Circle and passed the spot in the Chukchi Sea where they had had a near disaster on their last voyage. This time the *Nautilus* surfaced so that Anderson could get a better look at the chunks of ice that surrounded the submarine. Luck was with him, and he and the crew guided the ship through the dangerous channel.

Then, on August 1, the ship passed Point Barrow, Alaska, the northernmost settlement in the United States. In the deep Barrow Submarine Canyon, the *Nautilus* again submerged. The submarine was able to travel quickly and without difficulty in the deep canyon. Anderson listened to echo sounders which told him whether there was open water or thick ice above the ship. He and the crew also used underwater television to detect small pieces of ice in open water. At one point, the ship used its instruments to guide it over a 9,000-foot mountain range at the bottom of the ocean.

The route of the *Nautilus* under the North Pole

On August 3, the *Nautilus*, traveling at a depth of 13,000 feet, became the first ship to reach the North Pole. This event occurred just half a century after Commander Robert E. Peary and his five companions first reached the top of the world by an overland route in 1909.

After reaching the North Pole, the crew of the *Nautilus* had to continue under the sea to reach the Atlantic Ocean. Again, their master compass failed as they passed the spot where it had lost power on their first voyage. But this time they had an emergency power supply connected to it and the compass functioned correctly.

After carefully guiding the *Nautilus* through the deep, irregular channels under the Arctic ice, Anderson and his crew surfaced in the Greenland Sea on August 5. They had traveled more than 1,800 miles underneath the Arctic Circle. Messages from the *Nautilus* were sent around the world telling of their voyage. Then the *Nautilus* sailed to Iceland.

Anderson left the *Nautilus* in Iceland and was flown to Washington, D. C., where he received the Legion of Merit from the President Dwight Eisenhower. Four years after his voyage in the *Nautilus*, Anderson retired from the navy. He was elected to represent Tennessee in the House of Representatives in 1964. As a congressman, he has distinguished himself as a champion of civil liberties and the peace movement.

Robin Lee Graham

(1949-   )

People thrive on daydreams, especially when they are young. Young people seldom see themselves as "ordinary." They dream of accomplishments which will set them apart from the crowd. In the last 20 years, young people seem to be more aware than ever of the possibilities open to the individualist—the person who relies on his own judgment and instinct. Do any young people today still dream of a life at sea, of conquering wind and water alone?

Robin Lee Graham did. He, like his hero and forerunner Joshua Slocum, wanted to sail around the world by himself. When he was 13, his parents took him and his older brother on a sailboat tour of the South Pacific. Robin learned to navigate, to judge the moods of the wind and sea, and to keep a shipshape boat. In 1965, when he was only 16 years old, Robin decided that he was ready to make a journey around the world alone. His parents worried that he was too young to make the voyage, but they finally consented. They had, after all, encouraged Robin's love for the sea.

Robin in his sloop, *Dove*, at sea

A native of the Fiji Islands. Robin stopped at Fiji and many other exotic ports.

For the voyage, Robin's father bought a 24-foot fiberglass sloop, which Robin named the *Dove*. Robin and his father worked to make the *Dove* safe and seaworthy. The ship was equipped with a small outboard motor, a tape recorder, and a radio. Robin also studied trade winds and ocean currents.

Finally, Robin and the *Dove* were ready to begin. In July 1965, Robin sailed from Los Angeles to Hawaii, where his family lived. He stayed with them until September. Then, after saying final goodbyes to family and friends, Robin set sail from Hawaii with two kittens as shipmates.

Robin had not plotted his entire voyage because he wanted to be free to stop along the way and become acquainted with the people he was certain to meet. He was fascinated by the prospect of seeing distant lands and hearing foreign tongues.

But Robin was to wait through long days at sea before having the chance to see another human being. Only one week after leaving Hawaii, he began to feel his isolation. Loneliness plagued him throughout the voyage. Talking into his tape recorder helped, however. He dictated notes, records, messages to his family, moods and impressions. When he reached Fanning Island, his first stop, he sent the first of the tapes home. His family was always delighted to receive these "talking letters."

Robin sailed from Fanning Island to the Samoan Islands. He liked the Samoan natives and found them cheerful and friendly. They welcomed him into their villages and homes, and he feasted with them on fish, chickens, pigs, and yams baked in pits in the ground.

From Samoa, Robin sailed westward to the Fiji Islands, and then to Darwin, Australia. Robin stayed for two months in Darwin. He worked for one month to earn money for supplies, and he spent another month resting and repairing the *Dove*. When his ship was again freshly painted and seaworthy, Robin set out for the Cocos Islands in the Indian Ocean.

Like Joshua Slocum, Robin had excellent sailing conditions to the Cocos Islands. Brisk winds pushed him at least 100 miles a day, and he enjoyed the music of a chorus of crickets which had come aboard in Darwin. He also had time to make sandals, draw maps of the islands he saw, sew sails, and take snapshots of himself. Robin took the pictures by tying a string to his camera shutter and then pulling it while he was at the opposite end of his boat.

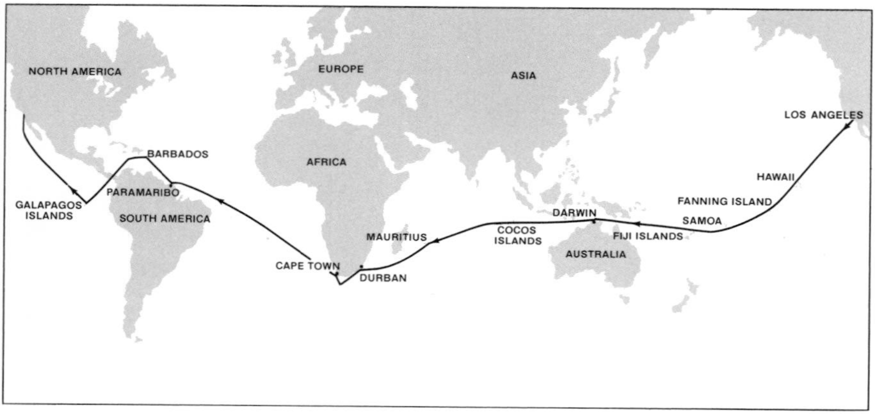

Robin's route around the world

Robin did not linger on the Cocos Islands. He took on fresh water and set out again across the Indian Ocean toward Mauritius, an island approximately 1,500 miles from the coast of Africa. The first night after leaving the Cocos, Robin was hit by a storm. Everything on deck that was not tied down was swept overboard. The mast holding the mainsail was broken and bent over the ocean. The safety harness that Robin always wore had to be removed because it was hooked onto the fallen mast. Robin tried desperately to get the mast and sail back in the boat. But then he was swept overboard himself. He had fallen into the sea without his harness. Luckily, he was able to grab the rail of the *Dove* and climb back aboard.

In the morning, Robin threw the broken mast overboard and raised a makeshift mast and a shortened sail. To increase the boat's balance and speed, he made another small sail from an awning and patched it with a dish towel and a shirt. Then Robin waited for a strong wind to push his almost helpless boat. For 20 days rough seas battered the *Dove* before it landed on the island of Mauritius.

Robin installed a new, stronger aluminum mast on Mauritius. He then set sail for South Africa. On the way he fought the heaviest seas of his voyage. The *Dove* nearly capsized several times. Loose objects were tossed about the ship and water sometimes leaked through the portholes. Robin was frightened and lonely, but he succeeded in reaching Durban on the coast of South Africa.

By this time, Robin had been at sea for over three years and he needed a rest from the punishing ocean. He found romance instead. Robin renewed a friendship with Patricia Ratterree, a native Californian whom he had met in the Fiji Islands. She was also traveling around the world. Robin and Patti fell in love. They rode Patti's motorcycle to a resort town on the coast and were married.

After his marriage, Robin found it very difficult to put out to sea again. He wanted to quit, but he felt that he had to continue. He had started something—something important—and he had to see it through.

Robin sailed around the tip of Africa in very bad weather and finally reached Cape Town. Patti had been traveling overland on her motorcycle and she met him there. Robin bought a two-way radio for the *Dove*, so that he could talk to Patti while he was at sea. She was to meet him in South America. Then Patti and Robin said a sad goodbye and he started on his lonely journey across the Atlantic.

Even though Robin could communicate by radio with his new bride, he still felt very lonely. Isolation was worse for him after enjoying the companionship of his wife. Robin found the days long and monotonous. He slept a great deal, and tried to read. But at times he felt that he might go mad.

Finally, after what seemed like an endless voyage, Robin reached Surinam, a small nation on the northern coast of South America. In Paramaribo, the capital, natives laughed at Robin's bare feet. They expected an American to wear shoes. Robin enjoyed a trip into the jungles of Surinam and a visit to a primitive Indian village, but he was eager to see his wife.

Patti arrived at last. She and Robin stayed in Surinam together for three weeks before separating again. This time Patti was to meet Robin and the *Dove* in Barbados, the easternmost island in the Caribbean Sea.

An Indian woman of Surinam in her dugout canoe

When Robin reached Barbados and rejoined Patti, the thought of continuing his difficult journey overwhelmed him. Again, he wanted to quit. But he decided that he could go on if he could get a larger boat. He felt that the *Dove* was too small and too old to sail another 5,000 miles. He flew to the United States and bought a 33-foot sloop with the help of the National Geographic Society. By this time, he was writing the story of his voyage for their magazine. Robin sailed the new *Dove* back to the Caribbean and to Patti. They stayed in the Virgin Islands for three months, waiting for the hurricane season to pass and looking for a buyer for the old ship.

Finally, Robin sold the old *Dove* and began the last part of his journey in the new boat. It had proven to be a fine ship in the voyage from the United States to the Virgin Islands. Robin sailed for Panama and passed through the famous canal. He was again in the Pacific and headed for California.

Robin comes home.

Robin and Patti had decided to interrupt the homeward journey one more time. They met at the Galapagos Islands, 700 miles west of Panama. Sailors of old called the Galapagos "the enchanted islands." They are full of strange beasts—giant turtles, seals, pelicans and cranes, and the only sea lizards in the world. Robin and Patti were delighted with these wild wonders. But again they had to separate. The final 3,000 miles lay ahead.

This last stretch of the voyage proved the most frustrating for Robin. The sea was calm for many days, and Robin made little progress. Finally, he hit favorable winds, and the *Dove* sped homeward. In April 1970, more than a month after leaving the Galapagos, Robin reached the end of his journey—Long Beach, California. He wasn't prepared for all the reporters and friends who swarmed aboard the *Dove* to welcome him home. He was the youngest sailor ever to have sailed around the world alone.

After five years of wandering over the oceans, Robin was happy to be home. He had recently learned that he was going to be a father, and he was anxious to start a new life with Patti. He wanted to attend college and someday build a house which would be close to nature and away from the crowded city.

"Would you do it again?" asked a reporter.

"Of course not," Robin replied. "Why do it again when you've done it once."